a **POP** of **COLOUR**

a POP of COLOUR

inspiring ideas to bring
colour into your home

GERALDINE JAMES

CICO BOOKS

LONDON NEW YORK

Published in 2020 by CICO Books
An imprint of Ryland Peters & Small Ltd

20–21 Jockey's Fields
London WC1R 4BW

341 E 116th St
New York, NY 10029

www.rylandpeters.com

10 9 8 7 6 5 4 3 2 1

A CIP catalog record for this book is available from
the Library of Congress and the British Library.

ISBN: 978-1-80065-039-8

Printed in China

Editor Annabel Morgan
Designer Toni Kay
Art director Sally Powell
Head of production Patricia Harrington
Publishing manager Penny Craig
Publisher Cindy Richards

For all photography credits, see page 172

CONTENTS

INTRODUCTION

When putting this book together, I was thrilled to be able to access so many wonderful images created by so many talented photographers and stylists. I have used them to demonstrate how to introduce easy, inexpensive and stylish pops of colour to any room, and I hope that this book will inspire anyone who has ever stood in the middle of a paint store bemused by the colour choice and thought 'HELP – where do I begin?'

Over the past decade, colour trends have been based around a grey palette. This has grown steadily darker, from dark grey to charcoal to almost black, and then expanded to include other dark colours, such as navy and forest green. But colour choice is intensely personal, and if a light, sunny, airy interior raises your mood, don't slavishly follow fashion and go for a dark grey bedroom with pops of neon. It won't make you happy.

So where does colour inspiration come from? So many places – plants, art, an item of clothing, Instagram. As I mention in the chapter on contrasting pops of colour, it was an oil painting that first set me off on a path to a kitchen full of green and turquoise. I'm not a matchy-matchy person, but colour links everything together.

I start off by talking about Pops of Contrasting Colour. The bold contrasts are not for the faint-hearted, but more subtle ones can be equally effective. Next, in chapter two, I show how tonal colour pops involve adding more of the same but in varying shades to build a considered scheme. Maximalists will be drawn to A Pop of Multicolour, which provides joyful inspiration for using all the colours of the rainbow. A Pop of Textile Colour discusses using fabric to layer in colour, while A Pop of Living Colour is all about choosing flowers or house plants to enliven your rooms.

But to start with, here's my list of ten fail-safe ways to bring exuberant, joy-inspiring colour into your home:

1. Add art. The bigger the better – bold, colourful and life-enhancing.
2. Update cushions/throw pillows or throws to ring the colour changes.
3. Introduce lots of living colour. Flowers and plants are nature's way of seasonally enriching your home.
4. Redecorate with a rug. Buy the biggest one you can fit into your space in a bold, punchy colour.
5. Paint a wall. To try out a colour, paint it onto a length of wallpaper lining, stick it to the wall with masking tape, then live with it for a week or so.
6. Can't choose one colour? Look for multicoloured wallpaper, cushions/throw pillows, bed covers and throws.
7. Paint a chair or stool. You can find inexpensive pieces at charity shops/thrift stores, online auctions and flea markets. Give them a facelift using leftover sample pots or spray paint.
8. Don't forget lampshades or lamps. They add not only another layer of light but a pop of colour too.
9. Collect coloured glass or ceramics. For maximum impact, decide on one colour and stick to it.
10. Use a mirror – again, as big as possible – to bounce all that lovely colour and light around your interior.

a POP of CONTRASTING COLOUR

1

Pops of contrasting colour are easy to add and make a bold statement in any home.

BOLD POPS

Friends often ask me for advice on how best to add colour to their home, and for as long as I can remember I've suggested they start with a simple pop of colour.

The good news is that this doesn't require a big investment in terms of time or money. A single glass vase in a fabulous colour can be all it takes to set you off. The starting point for my own colour pop journey was a painting containing the most rich, luscious tones. At the time, my kitchen was mostly white and in need of colour, and the standout colour in this painting was green, so I soon found a green pot to join it.

OPPOSITE Now this is the very definition of a statement piece. A two-seater sofa in cobalt blue leather jumps out against pale walls and speaks volumes about the owner of this home – surely someone adventurous and brave in their choices and unafraid to experiment.

ABOVE Beyond the stark white table and chairs, white sliding doors pull back to expose a dense blue hallway – an unexpected flash of colour in this cool modern space. A punchy mustard or orange would also work well used like this, as would a darker shade like forest green or slate grey.

Adding colour can inject fun and personality, and doesn't need to cost a fortune. A cluster of inexpensive paper lampshades, one of them a rich turquoise, enlivens this simple monochrome interior.

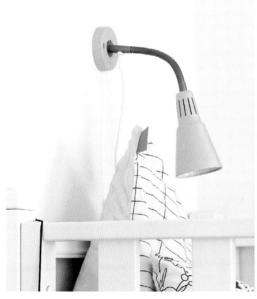

ABOVE LEFT Use lighting to add pops of colour to all-white interiors. A statement beaded Tiffany-style lamp in a very distinctive turquoise not only brings colour but also quirky detail to a white room.

BELOW LEFT A modern wall-mounted Anglepoise-style lamp in bold lemon yellow illuminates a top bunk.

ABOVE RIGHT This long plug-in light cord in bright primary yellow has been hung over a cup hook to light up a dining table or dark corner. It's a brilliantly simple way to add colour to an all-white room.

BELOW RIGHT A retro ceramic table lamp in dark green is boosted by the addition of a turquoise shade.

RIGHT You can use all sorts of accessories to contribute a pop of colour – posters, lampshades, rugs or cushions/throw pillows. These rich blue glass decanters, found at a vintage fair, bring a vivid splash of colour to a plain white mantelpiece.

FAR RIGHT This simple enamel pendant shade in a zesty lime is complemented by a wall sticker of a branch adorned with coloured baubles.

The pot soon became just one of a whole assortment of quirky green vessels and glassware that add both interest and colour to my space. A single item is all it takes to get the ball rolling – a poster, a lampshade, a cushion/throw pillow or even the cord on a lamp base.

Contrasting pops have perhaps most impact when they are used against a clean white or off-white backdrop, which acts as a cool, calm foil for a blast of bold colour. This can be a satisfyingly quick

LEFT If you've inherited a bland white kitchen, fitting a single block of colourful tiling is a simple and effective way to add some personality. This vibrant lime shade looks sharp against white cabinets and stainless steel. Tiny mosaic tiles like these ones come in sheets,so are easy and quick to apply.

OPPOSITE Repeated pops of the same colour are good for creating a sophisticated, pulled-together look. In this white kitchen, there are strong but sparing flashes of turquoise on the cabinets, seat cushions and even the artworks hanging on the wall.

LEFT It's not difficult to understand why a rich forest green was the choice for a colour pop in this converted warehouse apartment – it brings depth and contrast to the predominantly neutral interior while echoing and drawing in the lush verdant growth seen through the window.

LEFT A staircase runner or carpet is a brilliant way to bring vibrant colour to your home. Limiting the bold red to the stairs adds a luscious swathe of colour to this cool neutral scheme. Fitted carpets are obviously a significant investment, but if you confine them to one area, as here, they can completely transform a space.

BELOW LEFT This sums up the concept of a pop of colour so well. Taking pride of place right in the middle of a warm grey wall, a bold scarlet juju feather hat from Cameroon adds visual and textural interest.

OPPOSITE This polished hallway, with its David Hicks-inspired geometric wallpaper, is both classic and chic, but it's the dollop of bright red introduced by the two little chairs that brings it to life. Neon yellow or grass green would work just as well.

and inexpensive way to bring character and interest to a neutral backdrop such as a rental apartment where you aren't able to paint the walls. A plain white room can be injected with dynamism and energy with the addition of one item in a punchy hue. And once you get bored of your fire engine red cushion/throw pillow or retro orange lampshade, you can swap it for something new and exciting in turquoise or pink or lime green.

Of course, colour pops work equally well against a darker or more muted background. Neon leaps out against dark grey or navy walls, as does bright yellow. If you're ready for more of a

commitment, invest in a pot of gloss paint and tackle your mantelpiece or back door. The colour you choose may be based on a trend spotted in a magazine, or a shade that already features in your home. Finally, if you're more of a maximalist, try experimenting with equal colour contrast by setting your chosen pop of colour against a background colour that's equally vibrant.

OPPOSITE Punchy neons bring a vibrant energy and playfulness to any interior. They are particularly good used as contrast with darker backdrops, as shown here. A little goes a long way – note how a few touches of lipstick pink on the artwork and the quirky flamingo is enough to transform a sober interior into something edgy and rock 'n' roll.

ABOVE Again, a calm, warm grey backdrop is given a whimsical treatment thanks to a row of pink Russian dolls, pink pegs and other flashes of neon pink.

RIGHT Neon pink can pack quite a punch on a white background too. This restful bedroom is transformed into something quite different courtesy of an unusual artwork – a faded pink ball gown hung against a fluorescent pink background in an ornate gilt frame. No other colour pops required! I love unconventional art like this – I once decorated my goddaughter's room and adorned it with framed dolls and other precious items.

If you're only going to add one colourful thing to a scheme, it's a good idea to go for quirky or unusual – that makes the impact even more powerful. This twig-legged glossy red stool delivers a pop of interest and colour.

OPPOSITE A long bolster cushion in a vibrant orange leaps out against an ultramarine wall, creating a strong and sophisticated contrast. Orange is a cheerful colour, particularly popular during the 1950s and 1960s. The white plaster mouldings act as a headboard and offer some relief to this dramatic colour combination.

LEFT Yellow – the sunshine colour – is such a good choice to bring cheer. It can be overwhelming if not used with caution, but sparks joy when applied sparingly. Here, a tall spindle-back chair stands out next to the dark piano. A couple of extra bursts of yellow add balance.

BELOW LEFT The choice of yellow for this space is perfect – the pretty primrose shade on the door is echoed in the low bench for easy shoe changes. White tongue and groove walls are the perfect backdrop for vibrant pops like these.

BELOW A tiny seating area next to a window is ideal for five minutes of quiet contemplation with a coffee. The Patricia Urquiola Re-trouvé chair comes in many colours, and this zingy yellow is perfect against white, black and grey.

OPPOSITE Yellow is the right colour for a room divider, as it opens up a space, while the tall wirework floor lamp shows commitment to the theme. Although the yellows are all very slightly different, they harmonize well together.

Dark, intense shades add rich contrast, drama and warmth.

RICH POPS

As you'll see on the following pages, pops of rich, jewelled colour effortlessly introduce drama and indulgence to any room.

Many people find rich colours quite intimidating. They do make a bold statement, but use them in small doses and they will bring a sense of glamour and luxury to your home. In this section, I show the kind of adventures that these luscious colours can take you on.

Red is associated with passion and danger, and has connotations of

OPPOSITE AND ABOVE Dark velvet has all sorts of glamorous associations – it makes me think of the golden age of Hollywood, or old-fashioned gentlemen's clubs. Luscious dark blues and greens have become increasingly popular in recent years and they go so well with fashionable metallic finishes such as brass and gold. In both these rooms, the saturated blue of the velvet sofa is offset against dark walls and other rich tones and textures, while vibrant orange and warm yellows pop out against the opulent backdrop.

ABOVE LEFT Mustard yellow is an excellent hue for enlivening any dark interior. Here, the warm shade complements the brick walls, and the geometric cushion/throw pillow links the chair with a teal sofa.

BELOW LEFT Vintage tins and other kitchenalia in glossy fire engine red pop against rich teal shelves.

ABOVE RIGHT This intense Tiffany blue jumps out when offset with bright colours. The glossy red retro-style telephone adds a bold contrast.

BELOW RIGHT Orange brings a warm glow to a dark corner. Notice how the polished wood and the orange spines of the Penguin paperbacks increase the effect.

This dramatic statement takes my breath away. A chair as iconic as the Ovalia Egg chair by Henrik Thor-Larsen deserves a striking setting like this one, where the chalky turquoise walls emphasize the glossy white exterior and red wool padded interior of the piece.

wealth, status and prestige. Symbolizing good luck in many cultures, it delivers a punchy, dynamic pop in both light or dark spaces and is also a great mix with other strong colours.

I never used to be a particular fan of yellow for interiors, apart from a vase of humble daffodils, but I have a new-found respect for rich mustard and glossy primrose, and have already invested in a sample paint pot.

OPPOSITE **You don't often see much yellow in interiors, but it's a fantastic contrast colour, bringing energy and emotional uplift to a room. This galley kitchen with its sombre grey walls is given an unexpected burst of colour in the shape of a retro cabinet complete with its original handles.**

RIGHT **A plain wooden mantelpiece makes a bold statement thanks to a coat of glossy lemon yellow paint. How good it looks against the dark flamingo print wallpaper – and the zingy colour makes the stark black of the hearth really stand out.**

FAR LEFT AND LEFT **All shades of yellow look fabulous against a dark background, but if the thought of adding such a bold accent makes you a little apprehensive, you could have a trial run with smaller items such as stools, pouffes or even cocktail chairs. Vases, lamps and other decorative items are another quick way to bring some zingy colour to your space.**

ABOVE LEFT Paint your shelves the same colour as your walls and they will almost disappear, leaving intense contrasting colours to take centre stage. Here, a group of scarlet objects used as bookends leaps out against charcoal walls.

LEFT Dark walls provide a great backdrop for all types of art. This traditional gilt frame teamed with a strong raspberry mount brings the eye straight to the three images on display.

ABOVE Grabbing the limelight is this orange Artifort Mushroom chair by Pierre Paulin. The curvy silhouette of this renowned piece has a huge impact that's doubled by the bold colour.

OPPOSITE A navy or indigo wall is a very good alternative to dark grey or black. It will offer the same density and elegance but is not as hard. In this dark blue room, a velvet chair in a contrasting lemon yellow adds a mellow vibe that works so well.

LEFT Neon lighting is a brilliant way to bring a pop of colour and a playful flourish to any space. In this quirky home office, a neon wall light adds frivolity and fun. A vintage metal desk and Eames armchair complete the look.

OPPOSITE Entrance halls are the perfect place to experiment with bold colour contrasts, as they offer an intriguing welcome but are not a space in which to linger. The owners of this hallway tackled the narrow space head-on, using Farrow & Ball's Inchyra Blue on the woodwork/trim with a contrasting pop of yellow Babouche on the banisters.

RIGHT Setting a juicy apple green Vico Magistretti Vicario lounge chair against sanded floorboards and a warm blue wall with an undertone of violet shows great flair and decorative panache.

OPPOSITE This internal hallway has been painted in Railings by Farrow & Ball for a rich, cosy feel. The golden tone of the sanded floorboards is accentuated by the downlights, but it's the solitary red chair that gives life to this space.

ABOVE Whoever said blue and green should never be seen? How wrong they were. A cluster of vintage glassware in vibrant shades brings modernity to an elegant period mantelpiece.

Dynamic, extroverted orange is another warm colour and makes an excellent bedfellow with yellow and red, particularly when used as accents. And there are many glorious, regal blues, from cobalt to peacock to teal. Perhaps the biggest surprise for me is turquoise – it's so compelling and decadent, and in some of these rooms it's been used in ways that I would never have imagined. As I always say, if you love it, then do it. The rules are there to be broken…that's if you worry about those sorts of things!

ABOVE Riad El Fenn in Marrakech is famous for its sensational art, Moroccan crafts and bold colour contrasts. In one of the bathrooms, a brass-coloured bathtub exudes tremendous glamour set against a kingfisher blue wall. There's an exotic feel here that's heightened by the striking red and white striped stool.

Take a gentle approach and create light, airy interiors with a mood of quiet simplicity.

PASTEL POPS

Pastel colours are very easy to live with and shades of powder blue, shell pink, celadon green, Tiffany blue or primrose yellow are fresh, pretty and extremely restful, especially when teamed with white floorboards and muted walls.

Coastal homes often feature milky, washed-out aqua blues and greens combined with simple whitewashed tongue and groove walls. And the shabby chic lovers among us will always be drawn to faded shades, especially in the shape of vintage

OPPOSITE This sunny room in a whitewashed cottage beckons us to come in and take a seat. The two slightly scuffed and chipped vintage chairs add an invigorating pop of pistachio green that echoes the glass on the table holding flowers.

ABOVE This is such a simple but effective idea. The long curved hand rail on this staircase has been painted a cool minty hue that tones with the staircase. Paint offers many decorative opportunities and this is just one of them.

OPPOSITE Bubblegum, cherry blossom, putty – pink doesn't have to be relegated to a baby's bedroom. I like the character of pink, as it can be decadent or even slightly retro. Here, a cheeky artwork lifts a cool, glossy interior.

BELOW In a child's bedroom, a pink painted chest of drawers holds various treasures. The effect is fresh and simple yet still cosy and comforting.

ABOVE LEFT A pop of pink can be as transitory as a vase of pink flowers. Here, a Pantone mug holds a handful of pink pelargoniums from the garden.

ABOVE RIGHT Pink on pink. A candyfloss pink is framed with a paler shade on this cabinet, picking out the design features of the piece.

treasures, with their attractive patina and gentle signs of use. Mismatched pieces of second-hand furniture can be unified with a coat of a paint in a pretty pastel hue, as seen on these pages. And sprigged floral or gently patterned wallpapers will bring charm and additional depth to a feature wall.

Pastels aren't just pretty either. A couple of sugared almond shades – dirty pink or duck egg blue – will look sophisticated teamed with pale grey walls or set against a dark backdrop.

Informal yet stylish is the best way to describe this kitchen.
Care has been taken to balance the multiple toning shades of
blue and the overall effect is coordinated but not overdone.

Pink, pink and more pops of pink! This room mixes patterns and layers varying shades for a calm, warm yet energized mood that's ideal for a workroom or home office. The oversized dusty coral pendant light ties all the elements together.

Two retro spindle-back chairs have been painted sugar pink and peach, and provide contrasting pops of colour in this light, bright sitting room. This is a great way to update older pieces that are looking a bit shabby or old-fashioned.

OPPOSITE I love the way that reclaimed floorboards complete with their original worn and chipped paint have been used to clad one wall in this bright attic.

ABOVE A peppermint green enamel light shade with a slightly retro air sits well against pretty pink floral wallpaper.

RIGHT It's not just walls that can be painted to provide a pop of colour. Painting the woodwork/trim in a room is yet another possibility. Here, an original panelled door has been painted pale blue with the panelling picked out in a darker shade of turquoise.

a POP of
TONAL COLOUR

2

A colour pop using tones of the same palette will help you achieve a calm and relaxing modern look.

Simply put, a tonal, or tone-on-tone, colour scheme means you pick one main colour, then layer in as many different tints and tones of that colour as you desire. In a way, it is less challenging than adding contrasting pops of colour and the advantage is that the overall look and feel of a tonal interior is calm and relaxing.

Tonal schemes look sophisticated and fuss-free. If you stick with a monochrome look, you can layer

OPPOSITE **If you are passionate about a particular colour, a tone-on-tone scheme allows it to take centre stage. Although tonal palettes are often gentle and harmonious, this room positively zings with varying shades of pink, from watermelon to magenta. The wood calms it all down a bit.**

ABOVE **A zesty orange covers the walls and woodwork/trim in this hallway. The retro chair strikes a fun note, upholstered in a shaggy faux fur in a matching hue. The gloss-painted plant stand is bubblegum pink, which sits next to orange on the colour wheel and harmonizes perfectly.**

up black or white with all the grey tones in between. The same principle applies to any colour that you choose. If you decide upon blue for your main or foundation colour, you can use varying tones of that colour, from navy to powder blue, on the floor, ceiling, soft furnishings or accessories. Get hold of a paint colour chart and inspect it in pure daylight so that you can see all the different tints (the colour mixed with white) and shades (the colour mixed with black) of a particular hue.

ABOVE LEFT **More pink on pink in this interior. The walls are telling the main story, while the painting and fabric thrown over the banisters add more layers of colour.**

ABOVE **A pulled-back shot of the upstairs hallway shown on the previous page. Here you can see a light fitting in a tonal shade and that the staircase is painted a vibrant coral for maximum impact.**

OPPOSITE Riad El Fenn in Marrakech gives pink the modern treatment with this luscious peach wall providing a backdrop to an antique cherry-coloured velvet sofa.

While pink and orange are invigorating and energetic, dark tonal schemes such as the two shown on these pages offer a very different feel – one that is calm and contemplative. The sombre tones and assorted vintage pieces come together for a very modern look.

PAGES 58–59 There isn't much colour in this tranquil barn conversion, but multiple different tones of wood are layered together to create a warm, welcoming and relaxed atmosphere.

LEFT I love the vintage vibe here. Fresh pastel greens create a gentle retro feel that is enhanced by the bunting, the painted rustic chair and the fabric panels in the door. This scheme would be great for a cottage or small house with original features.

OPPOSITE Who wouldn't want to go glamping in this decommissioned vintage bus? The most wonderful space has been achieved using bright glossy yellow paint and toning vintage wallpaper. It's unexpected and really romantic.

Having said that, in this chapter you will see examples of tonal decorating that don't only involve paint colours. The different layers of colour in an interior may come from wood, art, soft furnishings and more. The important thing is that all these tones sit harmoniously together.

So how do you begin? The first step is to look for colour inspiration for your room. It may already be staring you in the face. Your main colour can be a strong one, as it plays a central role – I've based an entire scheme around just one boldly coloured throw. Do you love a particular

ABOVE Tonal shades from cream to peach to buttercup come together to create a sunny, glowing kitchen. You can see how a tonal palette is good for unifying very different features like the elaborate architectural mouldings and a modern wall cabinet.

ABOVE RIGHT Warm yellow works brilliantly with unpainted wood and washed linen textiles in tonal shades.

rug, painting, bedspread or even decorative item? That could end up being your starting point for a whole room. Be open-minded and you can have great fun collecting bits and pieces or even painting or spray-painting objects to work within your scheme.

Adding a pop of tonal colour doesn't have to be about a very polished or expensive interior – my ethos is all about achieving great results without serious financial outlay or having a team of experts on hand to advise. Instead, it requires that you understand the principle of tonal decorating, then implement it in a way that

suits your particular home and budget. So, for example, if you already have an old blue sofa, you might think about painting the wall behind a darker shade of blue, adding a throw or a couple of cushions/throw pillows that are slightly paler and arranging a couple of similar-coloured vases or books or any other objects on a shelf nearby. In this way, you are slowly but surely building up a tonal scheme. And it's this layering of similar shades that brings vibrancy and interest to any interior, especially if you're mixing different textures such as plush velvet and chalky paint.

ABOVE LEFT The pictures on these pages show how well wood works alongside warm, rich yellows. Here, the addition of a yellow-based olive green strikes a sophisticated note.

ABOVE The original 19th-century ceramic stove in this Scandinavian apartment provided inspiration for a tonal scheme based around warm putty shades.

LEFT I'd like to work from home in this sunny office furnished with iconic pieces such as the Bertoia chair. An unusual storage unit with drawers in graduated warm wood tones is positioned where it can be seen and enjoyed.

BELOW LEFT This squashy sofa upholstered in mousy grey-brown works well with the paler grey on the wall behind. The bronze vase and velvet cushion/throw pillow add a dash of luxe to the simple pairing.

BELOW AND OPPOSITE The full effect of the kitchen shown on the previous pages. Few of us live with such grand architectural detailing, but the combination of cheerful buttercup yellow, creamy sand and natural wood would translate well to any kitchen, whatever its size or style.

I love this modern monochrome look. A spectrum of greys has been used here, but despite the cool shades, a cosy vibe is the end result thanks to the textures of wood, sheepskin and linen.

ABOVE A white-on-white scheme is not for everyone, but it does create a dramatic and elegant effect. See how the stacked logs and the battered paint finish on the side table offer relief from all the white, as do the flowers and dried grasses.

ABOVE RIGHT Another monochrome palette. Again, texture brings softness to the scheme, and the tactile fabrics plus the ruffles on the cushion/throw pillow add a dash of femininity to the sombre shades.

RIGHT This tonal scheme extends the whole way through an apartment, from the lightest space in the foreground to the darkest tone in the room that's farthest away. This is a very harmonious way to decorate.

LEFT AND OPPOSITE Two rooms in the same home share a moody, seductive palette. The tonal effect of the dark walls and furniture is lightened by white painted floorboards and touches of gilt in the shape of a large circular mirror (opposite) and the dramatic brass palm tree lamps (left). This walk on the dark side won't appeal to all, but it certainly makes for high drama.

BELOW LEFT This inky blue bedroom is a masterclass in tonal layering, from the chalky blue-grey wall colour to the slightly paler linen bedding, the bedside tables/nightstands and the quirky blue pineapple lamps witih matching shades. Very cool and confident.

PAGE 70 This room is not really about colour – it's about texture. Yes, there are many tones of grey, but what really makes the space interesting are the contrasting surfaces, from the chalky walls to the faux fur throw to the wool sofa. It's all highly tactile.

PAGE 71 Dark charcoal walls, bedding and curtains are enlivened by the lustre of the tall brushed-steel cabinet and the glamour of the leopard print chair.

OPPOSITE AND RIGHT **Blue** has a calming and relaxing effect that makes it perfect for a bedroom. This one is very intimate and cosy, with walls and ceiling painted in rich, saturated swimming pool blue and ultramarine, and a matching quilt that boasts a dynamic zigzag pattern.

Tonal schemes work in any room, as long as you pick a main colour that suits the mood you wish to create. For a bedroom, you might opt for a duvet cover in a rich berry shade with an undersheet and pillowcases in softer shades of rose pink and a deep burgundy rug on the floor.

Another way of selecting a slightly wider yet nevertheless harmonious palette is to choose colours that sit near each other on the colour wheel – pale green, blue and grey, for example, or warm pink, red and orange. You'll still achieve a tonal effect, but it will have slightly more vibrancy.

THIS PAGE All the blues. Another blue bedroom proves that the colour makes for the most calming of sleep spaces. Here, sky blue walls have been paired with rich French blue washed linen bedding. The window frames are a darker marine blue, as are the chest of drawers and built-in closets. Slightly darker blue curtains and even a toning lampshade and base finish the look. The overall effect is so strong yet would be relatively easy to recreate. A scheme like this would work well to bring interest to a new-build home without interesting architectural features.

OPPOSITE Narrow wooden battens have been fixed on the diagonal to create an unusual panelled wall that acts as a headboard for a simple divan/box spring bed. The rich peacock blue colour is modern and sophisticated, and a few tonal blue cushions/throw pillows pull it all together. This would make an incredibly stylish teenage boy or girl's room.

OPPOSITE This children's room is perfectly balanced. A wall of practical built-in storage has been painted a rich teal blue, while the mustard velvet chair pops against it and the bold rug pulls everything together. The mood is both cheerful and calming for little ones, and it's a bit different to the usual pastels.

A feature wall is an easy way to enliven and add drama to any room in the house.

SINGLE WALL POPS

Feature walls are ideal if you want to make a decorative statement without committing to painting the whole room a punchy shade, which might be overpowering. Or perhaps you have some paint left over from a project that won't stretch to covering all four walls.

Of course, it takes a certain amount of confidence to make the leap, but the great thing about paint is that if you don't like it, you can just paint over it again! However, it is obviously going to

ABOVE The vibrant blue wall in this bedroom brings interest to a featureless small space that lacks architectural detailing. I love the small picture frame and bedside shelf painted to match, which really elevates the look. The colour is dense, but the pale green bedspread works well and doesn't fight the blue.

PAGE 80 This rich plum shade is quite an unexpected choice for country-style tongue and groove panelling. A wall with a fireplace is always a good contender for an accent pop of colour, as it will draw attention to an attractive period feature.

ABOVE LEFT These laminated doors in buttery yellow are vibrant and modern, and bring a sunshiny feel to a small kitchen. The turquoise table top contributes a further playful pop of colour.

BELOW LEFT In a narrow, dark stairwell, an accent wall can add interest and depth without closing in the space.

ABOVE RIGHT This shock of magenta pink has a real impact used in a pared-back urban interior. It contrasts in both colour and texture with the painted brick wall.

BELOW RIGHT Yellow, one of the primary colours, brings a charge of energy and positivity to a space. It's ideal for kitchens, utility rooms and other practical spaces.

LEFT I wonder what came first here – did the picture inspire the decoration, or was it the other way round? Either way, this is such an uplifting room – the strong primary brights have been brought together in striking coordination but are cooled down by the white ceiling and bedlinen.

OPPOSITE This bold crimson accent wall doesn't only add drama to a simple white kitchen – it also enlivens the view from the neutrally decorated open-plan sitting and dining room, which is perfectly framed by the doorway and the white wall. This is a brilliant solution if you've inherited a fitted kitchen that you don't love. Painting one wall in a luscious shade like this one is sure to distract the eye from less than lovely cabinets.

take time and money to create this effect, so there are a few things to consider before you crack open the paint pot and get busy with a brush.

First of all, make sure you choose the right wall – the idea is to highlight attractive features such as a period fireplace or an upholstered headboard in the bedroom. If you live in an open-plan space or studio, painting one wall can help define a particular zone – you could paint the wall behind the sofa a rich berry shade so that you're drawn there to relax, or choose sunny yellow for the wall behind a dining table for a family eating zone.

ABOVE This orangey tomato red has high visibility but is warmer and less challenging than a true red. It provides a brilliant backdrop to the inviting tableau of a toning easy chair and the elegant brass table lamp.

ABOVE RIGHT Like two old soldiers standing to attention in bright red uniforms, these vintage cinema seats tone perfectly with the wall behind.

When it comes to choosing colour, I have a few tips. Look at what you're working with. What colour are the other items in the room – furniture, curtains or blinds, upholstery and so on? You may want to opt for a wall in a darker shade of the same colour family for a sophisticated effect. If your space is already pretty neutral, you can introduce a strong or unexpected shade for an injection of drama. And what's going on outside the windows? If you look out over greenery, how about going for a darker green wall to increase the leafy, natural effect? If you're considering painting a wall that

divides a space, ask yourself whether the colour you like will work well with both rooms. This chapter is intended to provide you with plenty of inspiration and give you a nudge in the right direction.

Sample pots are a must. Buy a roll of wallpaper lining, cut large lengths, give them a couple of coats of paint, then fix to the wall with masking tape or adhesive putty. Live with a colour for a couple of days before making your choice. Finally, I would always suggest you paint the whole wall including the woodwork/trim - doors, window frames, skirting/baseboards and the mantelpiece, if it's plain wood.

ABOVE LEFT Choosing red can be daunting, so think about the mood you want to express in your interior. This pinky red brings a confident modern vibe.

ABOVE Statement walls are always effective when they highlight an existing feature in the room, such as a mantelpiece. This orange is a great background for a collection of retro 1970s-style ceramics.

ABOVE LEFT This wall demonstrates the finished effect if you colourwash rather than paint a wall – the colour is less dense and is gentler on the eye for a more relaxed feel.

LEFT In this pretty, cottagey entrance hall, a fresh, sunny yellow-green covers the wall beside the door. The other walls are a pale turquoise and the two shades are pulled together by the floral shoe bags hanging from a row of hooks.

ABOVE A citrus green wall adds punch to a narrow staircase. The shade needs natural light to bring it to life, as dark spaces can flatten this vibrant hue. The overall effect is very contemporary and also draws attention to the attractive modern white painted banisters.

OPPOSITE One wall in this room has been painted a soft aquamarine that would be perfect for a coastal home. The romantic mood is enhanced by very simple accessories – a bunch of flowers and some pretty vintage dresses.

Primary colours work well in children's bedrooms. This sunny, vibrant yellow is positive and uplifting, and the mood is joyful and playful. Notice how the sparing touches of powder pink soften the effect and add a calming note.

Of course, you can also choose to wallpaper a feature wall – and interesting wallpaper designs will add another layer of detail and depth. Here, a cheerful yellow provides the backdrop for a delicate bird and floral pattern, which adds charm to a simple whitewashed loft bedroom.

Experiment with imaginative and awe-inspiring colour combinations for a truly unique scheme.

COLOUR BLOCKING POPS

Colour blocking is painting certain areas of a wall or interior, or even putting together two or more different colours in one space. As you'll see in this section, it's a versatile way to add a pop of colour and a sense of personality to your interior. Again, it isn't a huge commitment because you can always cover the effects over with another coat of paint. It's also a fun way to use up any sample pots that you have left over from other decorating projects.

The first step is to decide which areas or walls to paint and how to introduce visual interest through

ABOVE A block of yellow gives a jolt of energy to any interior and a shiny finish adds intensity as well as reflecting the light. The natural wood floor, wooden beams and the painted green chair all work together to make the yellow feel earthy and warm rather than glaring.

OPPOSITE Big open-plan spaces need to be divided up into zones for different activities. This towering wooden room divider painted banana yellow seems a daring choice, but the solid block of colour makes the space come alive and brings the seating area a sense of privacy, despite the cavernous space.

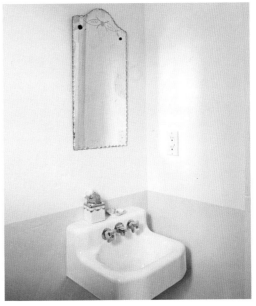

ABOVE LEFT Blue is a good choice for this narrow stairwell, leading up towards the light and ultimately the sky.

BELOW LEFT AND OPPOSITE This very graphic colour blocking is reminiscent of a Mondrian painting. Yellow and black have the highest contrast of all the colour combinations; that's why they yield such dramatic results.

ABOVE RIGHT This tiny alcove tucked in below a staircase packs a big punch in yellow – a ray of sunshine peeping out behind the white painted staircase.

BELOW RIGHT Colour blocking the lower part of a wall is easy, effective and practical. The pale blue against white is a fresh combination for a bathroom.

blocking. It may be that you already have architectural features such as skirting boards/baseboards, cornices/crown molding, picture or dado/chair rails that provide you with natural guidelines. Otherwise, I suggest using masking tape to mark out the areas to be painted (use a spirit level if you do it yourself, as wonky lines will spoil the effect). Don't forget the ceiling – often described as the fifth wall. If you have a very tall room, painting the ceiling a colour will make

LEFT AND OPPOSITE Coral pink and cobalt blue are an unexpected combination but work well together, probably due to the fact that the contrasting colours are equally dense and saturated. This effect is not for everyone but is incredibly modern and looks fabulous in photos. It would not be difficult to recreate it using MDF and wooden battens for the wooden panelling. The wall shelves have been painted the same colour as the panelling, but would also look strong if painted the same coral shade as the wall.

RIGHT A close-up of the geometric panelled wall. The ombre marble table is home to a Stoff Nagel candle holder.

FAR RIGHT A pair of Santa & Cole Cestita Bateria lamps stands out against the blue panelling – another example of the stylish contemporary design choices made when designing this space.

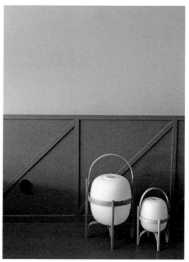

A brave up-and-over block of vibrant glossy tangerine adorns this wall and ceiling. The effect is decidedly retro thanks to the addition of the mid-century sideboard and bamboo lounger. This look would be easy to recreate with a ruler, masking tape and a small pot of gloss paint.

PAGE 97 In my opinion, blue and green should always be seen! They work so harmoniously together, as seen here. The owners have made full use of their curved stairwell, creating abstract blocks of colour that almost look like draped fabric.

LEFT A blast of glossy poppy red invigorates a sophisticated masculine interior and stops it from feeling dull or staid. It's a colour choice that injects warmth and works well with brown furniture.

BELOW More fiery red, in the bathroom this time. Obviously, this requires more thought and money than simply brushing on a coat of paint. However, tiny mosaic tiles tend to come in sheets, so are relatively easy to apply. And if you're going for budget white tiles everywhere else, a wall of lustrous colour really pops.

OPPOSITE The ceiling – the 'fifth wall' – has been used for a surprising and interesting block of colour in this minimalist kitchen. The magenta is bold but not oppressive, so it doesn't feel as if the ceiling is pressing down. This sort of scheme calls for good natural light and prevents the sleek modern kitchen from feeling sterile.

the space cosier and more cocooning. Or you could paint a broad stripe up one wall and extend it onto the ceiling to frame a large bed or a beautiful fireplace. Take a long, hard look at your space – there may be elements that are perfect candidates for colour blocking, such as window recesses, empty wall space, niches and nooks or other features that demand to be highlighted.

Now for your palette. Some interiors feature tonal blocking using different

This enormous room in a period apartment, with its stately high ceilings and big windows, has allowed the owner to think outside the box. It's the Mondrian effect again, but this time the rich orange and blue are broken up by the white painted woodwork/trim. You need a big, well-lit room to carry off these bold shades.

RIGHT A block of lime green tiles defines the shower area in this bathroom. Citrus brights in the shower work well, as they are believed to be invigorating. This shade would certainly wake you up in the morning.

BELOW An opaque window filters light into this tranquil room. The tongue and groove panelling creates a rectangle of warm lime that frames the statement bathtub. Pale blue walls are a good fit for a bathroom thanks to their connotations of sea and sun.

OPPOSITE Colour blocking with a difference. This is a clever and effective way to use two very different colours – by leaving a lot of white space in between them. The soft lime is complemented by the band of lilac and the tonal purple on the headboard – three colours that combine well in nature. Lilac is conducive to sleep, while lime brings vitality, so they are both good choices for a bedroom.

shades of the same colour, while others combine colours that you might not imagine would work together at all. It's important to clarify how the room is used – is it a space for peace and relaxation, or somewhere you require focus and energy? This will help you make the right choices. Alternatively, you might want to follow the latest trends or change things to suit the seasons. If you're only painting a small area, a sample pot may be enough, which will keep costs down. For a trial run, cut shapes from card or paper and paint each a different shade before sticking them to the wall. Enjoy experimenting!

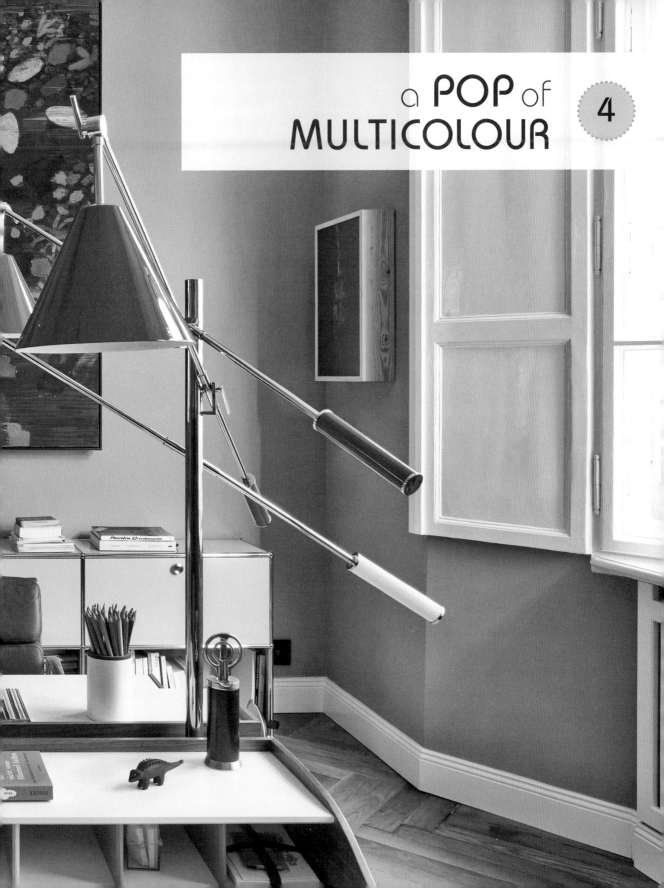

a **POP** of
MULTICOLOUR

4

Why tie yourself in knots choosing one colour when you can have many? If you're a maximalist, go ahead and create a bold interior with multiple pops of colour.

When I'm asked for my favourite colour, I find it impossible to answer. I think I have one…then I change my mind and move towards another. If you feel the same way, a patchwork of glorious colour may well be the way to go. Multicoloured pops of colour are a joyful way to create a beautiful home, and this chapter contains many ideas to inspire you. You may have a budding artist in the family, in which case giving them some paint and a wall where they can

ABOVE This room is a retro haven – and using all retro patterns means that the colours all belong to a certain design period and sit harmoniously together. Vintage fabrics and wallpapers can be easily found by searching eBay or Etsy, or scouring flea markets or specialist sellers.

OPPOSITE Bien Fait's bold Mosaic wallpaper is the perfect choice for a multicoloured feature wall and creates many opportunities to add toning colours. The rest of the room has been kept fairly neutral, but the carnival mood is accentuated by the addition of a vintage carousel horse.

This otherwise very simple kitchen has received the multicoloured treatment with most effective results. I like the use of the pale turquoise and peppermint green – a primary-coloured scheme would be a little bit too obvious.

ABOVE LEFT Multicoloured cone pendants hung at varying heights wake up this dark ceiling. The lower they are hung, the more they become part of the room.

BELOW LEFT The perfect way to mix up colours - the sliding doors on these cabinets and the back of shelves have been painted in complementary shades.

ABOVE RIGHT This is my favourite colour discipline - arranging my books by colour. Believe you me, once you start this process you will become obsessed.

BELOW RIGHT This snazzy tile-effect wallpaper brings vibrancy and colour to a bedroom wall. I love the way the single velvet cushion/throw pillow links to the pattern.

LEFT What a clever idea! Small boxes have been glued together to create a display unit for small ornaments, or in this case quirky figurines. The bases have been lined with vintage wallpaper scraps and pieces of wrapping paper for a multicoloured, multipatterned effect. The finished item is not heavy, so can be put up without using screws, perhaps with self-adhesive hanging strips.

OPPOSITE The frame of this internal window has been painted a jazzy yellow to bring a vivid dollop of colour to a white-walled kitchen. Further playful pops of colour have been added in the form of a door curtain, tablecloth and the vintage Tolix bistro chairs, but all of these can be swapped or removed at a moment's notice. I love the collection of different shaped and coloured vases and pots along the windowsill.

express themselves might yield interesting results – if you're brave enough.

Another option is wallpaper or wall art such as stencils or decals. The choice of multicoloured wallpapers is staggering and almost any effect can be achieved. Think about a scenic mural or,

perhaps, if that's too decorative, faux wood or marble in unexpected colours. This definitely isn't an amateur DIY skill, so you will need to find a good wallpaper hanger.

Very large pieces of art in bright and unusual colour combinations or an abstract painting

OPPOSITE These wonderful lofty floor to ceiling windows allow light to flood into this bright, airy room. The books are colour coordinated, two old armchairs have been brought back to life with blue velvet upholstery and the pop of fuchsia in the shape of the footstools is a great addition.

ABOVE An ideal scheme for a child's bedroom. All the cupboard fronts are different yet harmonious pastel shades, and the iconic Eames Elephant in pale pink gives the room the modern treatment.

RIGHT Children are attracted to bright block colours, like the ones in this cheerful nursery. While blue is supposed to be restful, orange is warm, comforting and cosy – perfect for a little person's bedroom.

LEFT AND OPPOSITE This geometric mural makes an unforgettable statement, although it's not for the faint-hearted. At first glance it seems to only feature primary colours, but there's also green and purple in the mix. The effect is big and bold, and has the courage of its convictions. The jewelled hues of the upholstered sofa cushions are the perfect finishing touch.

ABOVE A featureless, narrow staircase is brought to life with all the colours of the rainbow. It's a great way to use up old gloss paint – or to teach children the colours as you march up the stairs.

PAGES 116 AND 117 A brave approach to colour is evident in every room of this home, from apple green in the kitchen to cobalt blue on the bedroom walls. The dazzling mural was hand-painted by the homeowner. It's remarkable and slightly Ziggy Stardust in its look and feel.

encompassing all the colours of the rainbow can also do the job in one go. Choosing wallpaper or a piece of art means that someone else has done the work for you in terms of colour combinations and relieved you of the responsibility. However, colour does work very differently in different spaces depending on the light, so you may want to test out various colour combinations using sample pots of

ABOVE An old print tray has been given a makeover with its cubbyholes lined with colourful patterned wallpaper samples and giftwrap. Now it's a home for special treasures and brings cheerful colour to a child's room.

ABOVE RIGHT This rainbow-themed artwork could inspire you to create something similar using paint chips and a white display unit.

paint. You can also order wallpaper samples and see how they behave in your room.

If you're going your own way and adding multiple different pops of colour to one space, bear in mind that you will need some areas of white or another subdued tone to calm down the effect and prevent it from becoming too hectic or unsettling. This is especially true if you're using mostly primary colours.

A multicoloured rug is a good way to take your first steps. There is a wide choice available at well-known stores and at relatively low

prices. Rugs are instantly uplifting and, as with wallpaper, you can highlight certain colours by adding accessories in the same hue. Using a rug as a wall hanging will result in an effective design focus, and allow you to play with scale. Small rooms don't need lots of small things - large items look confident and impactful.

Adding accessories is something you can take your time with, as and when you see them. I am always saying take your time - there's no rush - but if, like me, you're impatient and impulsive, this might not work for you. I've never been one for practising what I preach!

ABOVE LEFT **A narrow alcove has been turned into a cosy nook for this vivid pink cot/crib. The colours of the bunting echo those of the hanging paper lampshades.**

ABOVE **Simple ideas are always the best. In this neutral interior, small squares of wood have been painted to create intriguing and colourful artworks that enliven a gentle workspace.**

If you've inherited a rather featureless kitchen or are renting, give it a lift by adding a few colourful accessories. These cheerful pots and assorted cooking implements bring warmth and personality to a utilitarian-style kitchen with white units and lots of brushed stainless steel.

LEFT Art and textiles are the best way to add instant colour and character to a room. Here, a traditional picture frame has been jazzed up with a lick of paint and used to frame a length of vintage fabric. A bright red bedspread covers the sofa, while the tablecloth contributes more pattern and a bold blue stripe.

OPPOSITE With a basic white kitchen, there are a few easy ways to inject a dash of personality. A baby pink Smeg retro refrigerator sets the right tone in this case, with the sunny yellow Ikea stool adding zing. Inexpensive bright blue tiles brighten up the food prep area and the whole scheme is grounded with the monochrome floor tiles. The result? A happy, functional and fashionable space.

PAGES 122–123 If you only have a couple of rolls of treasured vintage wallpaper, you'll have to be inventive when it comes to using them. The owner of this kitchen had the brilliant idea of using squares of retro wallpaper as a backsplash and covering them with glass. Open shelves, oversized lights and colourful accessories all add to the relaxed bohemian mood.

A very stripped-back monochrome scheme – white painted walls, ceiling and floorboards with a black chair and pendant lights – has been transformed from minimalist to multicoloured with the simple, easy addition of vintage textiles and painted furniture.

OPPOSITE Cole & Son's Prism wallpaper has a kaleidoscopic effect. Here it livens up a neutral space with wooden parquet and an oatmeal stair carpet. You could amp up the effect by painting the other walls in a lilac or yellow picked out from the paper.

We don't spend much time in a hallway, so this is the place to major on clashing colour if you're reluctant to have such bold hues in your living room.

LEFT Vibrant magenta walls and a collection of candy-striped framed artworks create a daring and sophisticated effect. You could replicate this wall of art with sheets of multicoloured wrapping paper in white or aluminium frames.

RIGHT This stunning mural provides Japanese cherry blossom all year round. I love the way it turns the corner and continues onto the adjacent wall.

BELOW These gorgeous multicoloured glass pendant lamps in rich, jewelled hues, some of them with decorative tassel trimming, make an unexpected addition to a green painted conservatory.

a POP of TEXTILE COLOUR

5

Using textiles to inject vibrant colour into your home is an easy solution, whatever your interior style. They allow you to express yourself by adding plain colour or pattern, whether it is neutral or bold.

Textiles are at the heart of every decorative style or trend I've used over the years. And, of course, the great thing about them is that if you want to refresh your room, you can just change the cushions/throw pillows, rug and curtains to create a whole new mood.

In this chapter, I discuss all types of textiles, from big investment pieces, such as upholstered sofas and curtains, to rugs and cushions/throw pillows – all of which can instantly transform a space.

OPPOSITE Although bright, this sofa is a mellow yellow, bringing sunshine to this glorious interior with its marvellous mural. Although a yellow sofa is undoubtedly a bold statement, it's also quite versatile and would look just as good set against a plain navy or white wall.

ABOVE On first seeing this pile of cushions/throw pillows, there appears to be multiple different colours, but on second glance there are actually two strong colour accents – turquoise and ochre – which are repeated to give a harmonious effect.

ABOVE LEFT Change your cushions/throw pillows with the seasons. These velvet ones in sumptuous jewel shades could be replaced with white linen during the summer.

BELOW LEFT If, like me, you collect fabrics for their patterns and colours, you will want to display them. I keep mine folded in a glass-fronted cabinet for all to see.

ABOVE RIGHT Don't forget fabric lampshades when it comes to adding colour. This sassy satin example brings additional va-va-voom to a pink bedroom.

BELOW RIGHT This is a brave fabric choice for a sofa, but the different colours in the design allow you to pick a couple out and use them for accessories.

The great thing about textiles is that you can use them to cover pieces of furniture for a quick facelift. Here, a patchwork quilt gives lots of opportunities for adding further pops of colour. The bold reds and blues are echoed in the retro print cushions. Notice how a variety of different cushion shapes and sizes adds visual interest.

The richly coloured, painterly fabrics featured on these pages are from Scottish brand Bluebellgray and this chair has been covered with their Butterfly print. It makes a fabulous trophy piece, but also notice the connecting thread of bright pink, which ties everything together.

FAR LEFT AND LEFT As I've said before, cushions/throw pillows are a good and relatively inexpensive way to add instant colour to any interior. These Bluebellgray examples offer a double dose of colour in the shape of a bold, loose print and a multicoloured bobble trim that echoes the colours used in the design.

RIGHT A contemporary sofa covered with a bold, romantic floral is a fresh and unexpected pairing, and the rich ultramarine paint on the walls balances the oversized print. Too cautious to plump for a dramatic fabric design? Recreate the effect by simply draping the sofa with a length of fabric of your choice.

In the living room, the sofa is the anchor of the space and dictates the style and mood of the room. I have had the same two cream linen sofas for the past 20 years, and they are a testament to the value and longevity of neutral pieces, allowing me to ring the changes with cushions, throws and other textile accessories. Having said that, I have had them recovered and, upon occasion, the seat pads refilled. This gives them a boost and a new

A riot of colour is not for everyone and if you need calm, serene interiors this won't work for you. But this picture tells me that the owner loves textiles and bright colours, and has travelled widely. Anchoring the room with a yellow sofa makes complete sense and ties the spicy colour palette together.

jurger &rs

mixed-media, ltd. chicago

LEFT In this room, textiles truly take centre stage. Look at the lampshade, the rug and the staggeringly beautiful Japanese-inspired bedspread appliquéd with birds and multicoloured flowers. The forest green bedroom walls are an unexpected choice, but the result is rich and glamorous, and I love that the mantelpiece has been painted the same colour as the walls, showing commitment to this opulent scheme.

OPPOSITE The natural world is the design inspiration in this home, with birds and animals on every surface, along with a taste for sumptuous textiles. Sitting on a rich wood floor is a large kingfisher blue velvet sofa – the perfect backdrop to the rich textiles. Touches of black and gold bring glamour, but the light walls keep this room fresh and sunny.

lease of life. But buying the fabric and paying for new covers is not quite as quick, easy and (relatively) inexpensive as changing the colours of your walls, so it does require some consideration.

I collect textiles myself and use them for decorative displays as well as practical purposes.

Over the years, I've amassed vintage linen sheets from flea markets and use them to cover my sofas and keep them clean. I also like to layer up my sofas and other seating with throws collected on trips to India or Morocco, where the textiles are as irresistible as sweets in a candy store – so vibrant,

ABOVE An attic bedroom beneath exposed eaves cries out for warmth and colour. The Aubusson-style rug introduces shades of raspberry and yellow, and these are echoed in the fringed bedspread and knitted throw.

ABOVE RIGHT A cotton voile curtain with appliquéd polka dots can bring colour to an all-white space or provide a colour reference to be picked up in the curtains, cushions or bedding.

daring and beautiful. In these countries, colour is used in such an expressive, dynamic way that I find it hard not to get carried away and buy everything in sight.

With a neutral base, creating pops of colour with textiles is easy. I've just acquired two burnt orange velvet cushions/throw pillows. These now have pride of place on one sofa alongside my vintage linen throws. I've changed the books on the coffee table to ones with orange covers and added a throw with an orange design to the other sofa. Hey presto – suddenly I have a rich autumnal look.

Curtains are another investment buy that require careful thought. In some rooms they are vital, whether to block the light or keep the room warm. If this is your situation, be careful of choosing anything too fashionable or matchy-matchy, as it may not stand the test of time. If you want to add pops of bold colour or pattern, go for less-expensive unlined curtains, which can change the look of a room without costing a fortune. As long as you have a curtain rail, you can hang almost any piece of fabric that's the right length with clip-on curtain rings, which have little pegs that hold the fabric.

ABOVE LEFT An array of sixties-style prints in pastel hues dresses a window seat. This would be a fresh but fitting look for a baby or child's bedroom.

ABOVE I love this idea – a headboard covered with quilted fabric for added cosiness, comfort and texture. If you fall in love with an expensive fabric, using it in small doses like this can have a big impact.

OPPOSITE Peeking through the banisters is a multicolour striped stair carpet – such a great idea. A carpet like this will make a family home so vibrant and joyful, and you can pick out any of the colours in the carpet and repeat them in the furniture and accessories. Here, a chair echoes the zingy lime and succulent pink, and pops against the white boards and walls. The whole space feels fresh and invigorating.

ABOVE The artwork is the starting point for a green and blue scheme created via a couple of bedspreads and an array of cushions/throw pillows. There's also a bold pop of colour in the form of the red-painted bookcase. The effect is informal but stylish.

RIGHT What a covetable display of richly coloured throws and cushions – the batiks, kantha and tapestry all work so well together. This gorgeous candy-coloured collection would look good in a sitting room or a bedroom.

BELOW Orange is a brilliant accent colour and works well in almost any interior scheme. Here, two cushions/throw pillows pop out against the dark green bench and decorative panel behind, and the vase on the mantelpiece continues the theme.

RIGHT A couple of standout cushions is sometimes all that's required to bring an interior to life, especially if you can track down dazzling colour combinations like these ones.

BELOW RIGHT These silk scarf print cushions from London-based brand Silken Favours would strike a note of glamour in any sitting room. If you're handy with a sewing machine, you could make your own covers from fabric chosen to work with your other possessions.

OPPOSITE This beautiful room uses textiles to bring rich colour and texture. The emerald green curtains and upholstered seating are covered in plush jewel-coloured velvet, while the cushions and rug introduce intriguing patterns.

Blue is a lovely colour to add to a bedroom. It's very calm and restful, even when used in a geometric pattern as here. I really like the pale blue colour block on the wall and this effect could be easily recreated in any room.

OPPOSITE Thick, luxurious curtains like these add a sense of luxury and are perfect for keeping the light out, but they don't come cheap. It's sensible to choose a neutral hue and then you can update the decor but keep the same curtains.

There are many quick ways to bring colour to rental homes where it isn't possible to paint the walls. A wall hanging such as a rug or bedspread adds immediate colour and texture to a space, and is a very effective way to cover an expanse of white wall. The grandfather clock case has been given a coat of tonal yellow paint.

BELOW A fuchsia cushion/throw pillow strikes a bold yet feminine note in a minimalist room. Simple but successful, the colour reminds me of my favourite lipstick.

BELOW RIGHT Fashioned from an old Irish linen glass cloth, this café curtain is a brilliant solution to the problem of screening a bathroom window. The blue stripes bring a breezy coastal vibe.

RIGHT I have always been a fan of using a beautiful piece of clothing as art, especially vintage items. This glamorous cocktail dress contributes a pop of vibrant red in a bright, airy space. Displaying treasured garments is such a quick and easy way to add colour.

Bring instant joy
and an abundance
of colour to your
home with plants
and flowers.

I love to have flowers in my home
at all times – they bring me so much
pleasure. They are the finishing
touch to any interior decoration
or display, whether a riot of
bright tulips or whole branches
of blossom that I've hauled in
from the big tree in my garden.

Plants and flowers can bring
shape and height, fill an empty
corner or enhance a table setting
and even set the tone for the
season. A poinsettia might signify

OPPOSITE Big, bright blowsy
gladioli tone with the red colour
pops in this hallway. These
showy, long-stemmed flowers
suit a tall vase and are good
value for money too, generally
lasting about a week.

ABOVE Under this vintage
photograph of a sailor,
individual vessels holding
single stems bring to life
the austere black and white
photograph. This effect is
easy to recreate with an
assortment of small glass
vases and a few flowers from
the garden, if you have one.

ABOVE LEFT Fragile poppies with sinuous stems seem to take on a life of their own against a dark background.

BELOW LEFT Just as pastel rooms are easy to live in, pastel flowers are easy to live with. These sugar pink hydrangeas in a lacy vase are so feminine and pretty.

ABOVE RIGHT Purple-blue hydrangeas and tulips are in perfect harmony on this wooden table. Both are easily available from florists or even the supermarket.

BELOW RIGHT Lovely lupins in various shades of lilac have an almost vintage feel. A simple glass bottle vase is all that's needed.

It's a bit of a cliché, but sometimes less really is more, as with this beautifully composed mantelpiece. The calm arrangement of two modern vessels and antique china plus a jug holding three blowsy peonies has the air of a still life painting.

These are party flowers with a difference. Instead of huge formal arrangements, go for multicoloured pops with lots of different jewel shades in equally vibrant vases arranged on a white painted staircase.

OPPOSITE Wow, wow and more wow! What a clever use of a vintage wooden bottle rack. Fix glass test tubes or other tiny watertight containers to hold a huge array of real (or faux) multicoloured flowers to create an epic display.

LEFT A narrow console table in a light, bright room is the perfect place for your own little botanical garden. These house plants are all fairly robust, so good for beginners. The print of different varieties of melon hanging on the wall behind continues the botanical theme.

BELOW Lush house plants mixed with books and etymological prints give a vintage greenhouse feel.

OPPOSITE An old baker's or lab trolley displays a selection of leafy ferns, cut flowers and other house plants. You could recreate this effect by filling a smaller trolley (Ikea does a good one) with your choice of house plants. Keep it somewhere with plenty of humidity, like a bathroom.

Christmas, while the arrival of tulips heralds spring and then the roses appear in early summer. Nothing speaks louder than a good old bunch of daffodils to say that winter is over and sunshine is on its way again. Red roses signal romance, while the huge bouquets sent to celebrate anything from birthdays to the arrival of a new baby will make a colourful statement in any home. Flowers bring fragrance too – think of the heady perfume of tuberose or the delicate scent of lily of the valley.

Using flowers in the same colour as your interior decor or textiles is easy on the eye. In this bedroom, a big bunch of pinky purple delphiniums sits tall on a bedside table.

ABOVE So simple but so effective. Hydrangeas are one of my favourite flowers because of their versatility and their unique colours. This faded blush pink variety echoes the colours in the artwork behind.

ABOVE RIGHT The season for gladioli seems to come and go so quickly, but when they are available, they are very good value for money. Displaying them as single stems in simple glass bottles extracts maximum impact from these graceful and exotic beauties.

RIGHT In another example of cut flowers echoing the colour scheme of an interior, this pretty, loose and rustic arrangement has almost a raspberry ripple effect, with darker purple studding the pale pink.

An assortment of cut flowers, succulents and house plants in simple, sturdy containers creates a lively, colourful and interesting display. The botanical bunting hanging on the wall behind adds another layer of detail.

I tend to buy flowers in quite specific colours because I know they suit particular rooms in my house. However, sometimes I need a change and then I pick a contrasting colour deliberately to make an impact. Big blowsy hydrangeas offer volume and come in a wide range of colours – the brightest of pinks or dreamy sky blue. They also dry beautifully, so are long-lasting. I like my flowers to make a statement and I often go for large or long-stemmed varieties to create tall displays, such as branches covered with red berries at Christmas or blossom in springtime.

OPPOSITE In a neutral interior, house plants bring a glorious rich green pop of colour as well as a feeling of life and energy. Even the smallest and simplest of temporary apartments, student digs and rental properties will feel like home once a few plants have been introduced to the interior.

ABOVE LEFT A sunny windowsill is the perfect home for house plants, as it creates greenhouse conditions. Don't forget to mist and water plants regularly if they are situated near a radiator – half-dead plants are not a good look.

ABOVE RIGHT I like the homeowner's ingenuity here, creating storage and display space from empty crates and a narrow stool. This is a great idea if you have limited space or are on a tight budget.

LEFT Sumptuous, luscious plants grab all the attention here, and their hues are echoed in the green painted wall and cabinet set off by a pop of orange in the shape of the chairs. One word of warning – if you want to recreate this effect, make sure you can access hanging plants in order to water them.

OPPOSITE Another view of the same interior. The deep, generous velvet sofa and oversized ottoman show real commitment to the leaf green theme. The overall effect here is of living in a greenhouse – one can hardly tell where the inside stops and the outside begins.

The recent trend for plants and biophilic living, or living connected to nature, is hugely exciting. House plants are not only on trend, they will also introduce accents of nature's greatest colour, calming, harmonious green, into your living space. If that wasn't enough, a famous NASA study discovered that certain house plants are effective at removing pollutants from the air. And caring for plants can reduce psychological stress. In all, living with plants is beneficial on every level. So take inspiration and bring living colour pops into your home – they are true life enhancers.

RIGHT Amaryllis 'Minerva' is a resplendent flower known as the Christmas star. Its spicy red flowers with a splash of white look great in simple glass containers.

BELOW Simple but effective – a narrow red vase holds three anemones, offset by a white curtain with red dots.

ABOVE Three low vases hold a collection of exotic orange and red flowers. I love vibrant mixtures of different blooms and this cluster is just the right height for a table arrangement.

Red is the colour. Here, a shiny round red vase holds bright red roses. Displaying roses at an angle adds a touch of theatre. The flowers are balanced with a red cushion/throw pillow and the slim red book on the coffee table.

SOURCES

PAINTS

Annie Sloan
anniesloan.com
Easy to use decorative furniture paint that can be applied to almost any surface.

Farrow & Ball
farrowandball.com
This brand is a long-time favourite of so many of us; well-trusted and always adding inspirational colours. In 2010, they made the decision to move to an entirely eco-friendly water-based range of paints with low VOC (volatile organic compounds).

Little Greene
littlegreene.com
A wide range of both traditional and modern paints, including a Colours of England palette with historical references.

Mylands
mylands.com
One of the oldest family-run paint companies, dating back to 1884. It has good eco-credentials and offers a vast range of beautiful colours.

FLOWERS AND PLANTS

Most large cities have a wholesale flower market. Local independent florists will also have a selection of flowers and plants, and if you're venturing to Ikea, it has a good-value offering of house plants.

Columbia Road Flower Market
columbiaroad.info
A vast collection of seasonal flowers and plants to brighten and fill your home.

New Covent Garden Market
newcoventgardenflowermarket.com
The place to go if you want to bulk buy flowers and plants.

Scarlet & Violet
scarletandviolet.com
One of my favourite florists, with an emphasis on colour and scent. I love the loose, informal, almost rustic aesthetic.

Wild at Heart
wildatheart.com
Nikki Tibbles is one of the most visionary florists in London.

TEXTILES

Bluebell Gray
bluebellgray.com
Scottish design studio selling the most vibrant, uplifting and colourful cushions, bedlinen and curtains.

Caravane
caravane.co.uk
A French company selling an array of sumptuous cushions, throws and other accessories in interesting colours and patterns.

Design Centre Chelsea Harbour
dcch.co.uk
Over 120 showrooms and 600 of the world's prestigious brands.

Designers Guild
designersguild.com
Inspirational fabrics, cushions and wallpapers with the most expressive use of colour.

Etsy
etsy.com
Affordable and unique with a wide range of everything and anything, including vintage fabrics. I particularly love the African wax prints.

Society Limonta
societylimonta.com
Premium quality pure linen in a wide range of colours for both bed and table.

Soho Home
sohohome.com
A range of homewares inspired by the Soho House hotels and including lovely jewel-coloured velvet cushions, perfect for adding a pop of colour.

HOMEWARE RETAILERS

Anthropologie
anthropologie.com
A beautifully curated home collection of cushions, furniture and accessories.

Design Vintage
designvintage.co.uk
Scandinavian living. Trendy home accessories, including art, and furniture plus rugs.

H&M home
hm.com
A large selection of designs at extremely keen prices, perfect for updating your home or adding a pop of colour. Good range of affordable bedlinen.

Home Barn
homebarnshop.co.uk
Full to the brim with exciting vintage and antiques mixed with quirky accessories.

Ikea
ikea.com
Affordable furniture and accessories – pick up ordinary pieces to paint and add a pop of colour to your home. Also a wide range of colourful rugs.

A New Tribe
anewtribe.co.uk
An independently owned shop filled with appealing objects and a vast selection of rugs from Morocco, as well as contemporary designs.

Petersham Nurseries
petershamnurseries.com
A destination of beauty, here you will find a collection of carefully selected gifts and accessories, plants and pots, all showcased in old Victorian greenhouses set among the meadows of Petersham.

ART
Affordable Art fair
affordableartfair.com
Wide range of well-priced art from independent artists, and a good place to see a varied selection of styles.

Art finder
artfinder.com
An online marketplace for a huge range of well-priced art from all over the world.

BetterShared
bettershared.co
Vibrant contemporary African art.

King & Mcgaw
kingandmcgaw.com
Inspiring art for your home, from rare and limited prints to black and white photography.

Paper Collective
papercollective.com
Graphic prints produced in Denmark using only FSC (Forest Stewardship Council) materials and certified sustainable. They have a section devoted to colourful art.

WALLPAPER
Cole & Son
cole-and-son.com
Beautiful luxury hand-blocked papers, including some fine historic papers and quirky modern designs.

Matthew Williamson
matthewwilliamson.com
Wallpaper and fabrics in a rainbow of hues from this British fashion designer-turned-interior designer, known for his exciting use of vibrant colour.

Wallpaper Direct
wallpaperdirect.com
A one-stop shop for wallpapers, perfect for creating a wow wall.

PHOTOGRAPHY CREDITS

1 Debi Treloar; 2 Jan Baldwin; 3 Rachel Whiting; 4–5 Beth Evans; 6 above left, above right and below left Catherine Gratwicke; 6 below right Jan Baldwin; 8 Katya de Grunwald; 9 Polly Wreford; 10–11 Polly Wreford; 12 Katya de Grunwald; 13 Maíra Acayaba; 14 Polly Wreford; 13 above left and above right Catherine Gratwicke; 13 below left Rachel Whiting; 13 below right Polly Wreford; 16 above left Polly Wreford; 16 above right Rachel Whiting; 16 below Katya de Grunwald; 17 Polly Wreford; 18–19 Maíra Acayaba; 20 above Jan Baldwin; 20 below Polly Wreford; 21 Polly Wreford; 22 Susie Lowe; 23 both Rachel Whiting; 24 and 25 Polly Wreford; 26 above Catherine Gratwicke; 26 below left Debi Treloar; 26 below right Polly Wreford; 27 Katya de Grunwald; 28, 29, 30, 31 and 32 all Catherine Gratwicke; 33 above Debi Treloar; 33 below left Catherine Gratwicke; 33 below right Polly Wreford; 34 above left Polly Wreford; 34 above right Catherine Gratwicke; 34 below left and 35 Debi Treloar; 36 Catherine Gratwicke; 37 above neon light from bagandbones.co.uk; 37 below Beth Evans; 38 Jan Baldwin; 39 above left Polly Wreford; 39 above right Catherine Gratwicke; 40 and 41 Catherine Gratwicke; 42 Susie Lowe; 43 above left and below Catherine Gratwicke; 43 above right Susie Lowe; 44–45 Simon Brown; 46 Catherine Gratwicke; 47 Debi Treloar; 48 and 49 Catherine Gratwicke; 50–51 Beth Evans; 52–53 Catherine Gratwicke; 54 left Claire Richardson; 54 right Catherine Gratwicke; 55 Catherine Gratwicke; 56 and 57 Beth Evans; 58–59 Debi Treloar; 60 Catherine Gratwicke; 61 Debi Treloar; 62, 63, 64 and 65 Beth Evans; 66 Catherine Gratwicke; 67 above left Polly Wreford; 67 above right Lisa Cohen; 67 below Jan Baldwin; 68 and 69 Debi Treloar; 70 Dan Duchars; 71 Debi Treloar; 72, 73, 74 and 75 Beth Evans; 76–77 Maíra Acayaba; 78 Rachel Whiting; 79 Catherine Gratwicke; 80 Chris Everard; 81 above left, above right and below right Debi Treloar; 81 below left Christopher Drake; 82 Debi Treloar; 83 Rachel Whiting; 84 left Chris Everard; 84 right Catherine Gratwicke; 85 left Beth Evans; 85 right Catherine Gratwicke; 86 above left Debi Treloar; 86 above right Simon Brown; 86 below left Catherine Gratwicke; 87 Debi Treloar; 88 Rachel Whiting; 89 Debi Treloar; 90 Jan Baldwin; 91 Katya de Grunwald; 92 Polly Wreford; 93 above left Ray Main; 94 above right Rachel Whiting; 94 below left Polly Wreford; 94 below right Amy Neunsinger; 94 and 95 Beth Evans; 96 Rachel Whiting; 97 Catherine Gratwicke; 98 and 99 Chris Everard; 100–101 Jan Baldwin; 102 Polly Wreford; 103 and 104–105 Jan Baldwin; 106 Debi Treloar; 107 Rachel Whiting; 108 Simon Brown; 109 above left and right Simon Brown; 109 below left Debi Treloar; 109 below right Catherine Gratwicke; 110 Emma Mitchell; 111 Debi Treloar; 112 Simon Brown; 113 above Maíra Acayaba; 113 below Rachel Whiting; 114 and 115 Debi Treloar; 116 and 117 Catherine Gratwicke; 118 left Rachel Whiting; 119 right Simon Brown; 120 left Debi Treloar; 120 right Emma Mitchell; 120 above Maíra Acayaba; 120 below Claire Richardson; 121 Rachel Whiting; 122–123 Debi Treloar; 124 Debi Treloar; 125 Susie Lowe; 126 Emma Mitchell; 127 above left Chris Everard; 127 below left from shed style; 127 below right Rachel Whiting; 126–127 Rachel Whiting; 130 Catherine Gratwicke; 131 Rachel Whiting; 132 above left Polly Wreford; 132 above left and below right Debi Treloar; 132 below right Catherine Gratwicke; 133, 134 and 135 all Debi Treloar; 136–137 Rachel Whiting; 138 and 139 Catherine Gratwicke; 140 left Katya de Grunwald; 140 right Debi Treloar; 141 left Debi Treloar; 141 right Maíra Acayaba; 142 Jan Baldwin; 143 above Debi Treloar; 143 below Rachel Whiting; 144 left Catherine Gratwicke; 144 above right Lisa Cohen; 144 below right and 145 Catherine Gratwicke; 146 Rachel Whiting; 147 Polly Wreford; 148 Katya de Grunwald; 149 above right Debi Treloar; 149 below left Simon Brown; 149 James Merrell; 150–151, 152 Catherine Gratwicke; 153 Paul Massey; 154 above left Debi Treloar; 154 above right Andrew Wood; 154 below left and right Debi Treloar; 155 Simon Brown; 156 Jan Baldwin; 157 Catherine Gratwicke; 158 and 159 Rachel Whiting; 160 Catherine Gratwicke; 161 above left Tom Leighton; above right Rachel Whiting; 161 below right Emma Mitchell; 162–163, 164 and 165 Rachel Whiting; 166 and 167 Catherine Gratwicke; 168 above Emma Mitchell, below left Simon Brown, below right Catherine Gratwicke; 169 Catherine Gratwicke; 171 Rachel Whiting; 173 Polly Wreford; 174 Catherine Gratwicke; 176 Jan Baldwin.

INDEX

ACKNOWLEDGMENTS

Thank you to Cindy Richards, the publisher of CICO Books, for commissioning me to write this book. Thank you also to Annabel Morgan, for her gentle encouragement and support with words, and to Toni Kay, who, as always, did a wonderful job on the design.

Thank you to all the authors, photographers, stylists and homeowners who provided such outstanding content drawn from a huge library of wonderful images to illustrate the book.

Finally, as always, thank you to my daughter Rosie, for her unstinting support and help.